ORPHANS

D1425194

Dennis Kelly

ORPHANS

OBERON BOOKS
LONDON

WWW.OBERONBOOKS.COM

First published in 2009 by Oberon Books Ltd
521 Caledonian Road, London N7 9RH
Tel: +44 (0) 20 7607 3637 / Fax: +44 (0) 20 7607 3629
e-mail: info@oberonbooks.com
www.oberonbooks.com

Reprinted 2010 (twice), 2011, 2012

A catalogue record for this book is available from the British
Library.

ISBN: 978-1-84002-943-7

Printed and bound by CPI Group (UK) Ltd, Croydon, CR0 4YY.

Characters

HELEN

DANNY

LIAM

I'd like to thank Matthew Dunster, David Lan, Tessa Walker, Ben Payne and Mel Kenyon for their help with this script. But most of all I'd like to thank Rox, for once again being tough as fuck and not letting me get away with anything.

Birmingham Repertory Theatre Company and Traverse Theatre Company in association with Paines Plough present *Orphans* by Dennis Kelly, first performed on 31 July 2009 at the Traverse Theatre, Edinburgh with the following cast:

LIAM	Joe Armstrong
HELEN	Claire-Louise Cordwell
DANNY	Jonathan McGuinness

Director	Roxana Silbert
Designer	Garance Marneur
Lighting Designer	Chahine Yavroyan
Sound Designer	Matt McKenzie
Assistant Director	Ben Webb

Stage Manager	Paul Southern
Deputy Stage Manager	Martin Hinkins
Assistant Stage Manager	Naomi Stalker

ONE

HELEN and DANNY's flat.

A candlelit dinner, interrupted.

HELEN dressed up, DANNY dressed up.

LIAM stands there having just come in.

He has blood all down his front.

Pause. They stare at him.

For a long time.

LIAM   Alright, Danny?

DANNY   Liam.

LIAM   Helen.

HELEN   Liam.

         Pause.

LIAM   How's it –

         How's it going, like, you alright?

DANNY   What? Yeah.

         Pause.

         You?

LIAM   Yeah. You know.

         Beat.

         Not too, er…

         You know.

DANNY   Right.

         Pause.

LIAM   Nice dress.

HELEN   What?

LIAM   Nice dress.

       Beat.

       Is it new?

HELEN   Is it new?

LIAM   Yeah, is it, like

HELEN   Is my dress new?

LIAM   Yeah, is it –

HELEN   Yes. It's new, Liam.

       It's a new dress.

LIAM   It's nice, it's sort of –

       It's one of those…

       Beat.

       You having dinner? Where's Shane?

DANNY   He's at my mum's.

LIAM   Right. Nice. So you're having like a

DANNY   Yes.

LIAM   what, like celebratory, celebrating

DANNY   What?

LIAM   like a romantic

DANNY   Yeah.

LIAM   What's that, salmon?

HELEN   You're covered in blood, Liam.

LIAM   Yeah. Sorry about that.

       Beat.

It's this lad's.

HELEN   This lad's?

LIAM   Yeah, it's this lad's

DANNY   What lad's?

LIAM   blood, it's this lad's.

DANNY   Are you alright?

LIAM   Yes. Yes, thank you, Danny, I am alright. Sorry. You
             should go back to your, it looks nice, is that your, is
             that your basmati…?

DANNY   Yeah, it's

LIAM   Yeah, it's not mine, it's this lad's blood. This poor
             fucking, just this poor lad's.

HELEN   Has there been an accident?

LIAM   Coming in like this, and you're having a dinner, like
             a celebratory

DANNY   It's okay, don't worry, it's alright

HELEN   Has there been an accident, Liam?

LIAM   You do that, you do that, did you do that with
             lemon and olive oil, Danny? That rice you do, I
             love that, bit of the old cracked…?

HELEN   So there has been an accident?

LIAM   and I'm walking in like some sort of, some sort of
             fucking…

HELEN   What sort of accident?

DANNY   Helen, please…

LIAM   It's gonna get cold, get all cold, Danny it's gonna
             get all fucking –

             Beat.

I come round the corner and he's

like, on the

fucking

lying, on the pave–, on the tarmac, on his own.

He's lying there on his own and I thought 'ah, no. Ah fuck, ah no, he's on he's own. He's on his fucking own.' And he was like an ordinary, Danny, you know, just like I don't know, I mean he looked like a decent, he looked, alright fair enough, maybe a bit you know, but like you'd have a drink with him though, I mean not necessarily a friend, but you might in a pub or something, if you just, if you just met, game of pool, a pint with, a decent pint with, am I rambling? I am, aren't I, I'm rambling, talking shit, fucking talking shite, and now he's lying there on his own, completely on his own. With blood. And like, and someone has…

some fucking…

someone has really –

> *Suddenly overcome.*

> *They watch.*

HELEN   So what, there's been an accident, then?

DANNY   Jesus Christ, Helen!

HELEN   I'm just asking, Danny! I'm just trying to clarify –

DANNY   He said it's not an accident

HELEN   When? he didn't say… Liam, you didn't say

DANNY   He did, he did say, he just said

HELEN   He did not say that it was not –

LIAM: That wasn't an accident.

She says nothing.

DANNY   D'you wanna drink?

LIAM   No thanks, could I have a glass of wine?

DANNY gets him some wine.

This country. It's just…monsters and… It's dark out there.

Sorry I didn't knock, I used the key. I know it's just, emergencies and stuff but I thought this might actually be a bit of a, you know, and I was thinking what if I knocked, Hels? and you see me it's like shock, someone like this, covered, but how do you not shock when you're covered, and then I panicked coz the door slams, that door, if you let it go, doesn't it, Danny, if you let it go it slams back, so I was gonna call out, but then I thought you'd shit your fucking bricks, and in your, Hels, you know, condition and what have you, you don't need to shit your fucking bricks in your condition and I don't mean that to sound in a patronizing way, coz it's not like you're ill, you're not ill, or like you're ill or something, it's not like that, but still if you heard someone in the hall shouting out you would just shit your fucking, and that is not right. So I've been out there for about fifteen minutes really, not really knowing what to…you know…

do.

HELEN   Liam, I want you to look at me.

LIAM   Yeah.

HELEN   Look at me.

LIAM   I am looking at you.

HELEN   Look at me.

LIAM   Okay.

HELEN   I want you to think. And I want you to tell me. Who's blood is this.

       Pause.

LIAM   I tried to help him.

       DANNY gives him his drink.

DANNY   The lad on the tarmac?

LIAM   Yeah, the lad on the tarmac, and he's been hurt

DANNY   By who?

LIAM   By people.

HELEN   By what people?

LIAM   I dunno. I dunno what people. He was bleeding.

HELEN   Where was he bleeding from?

LIAM   Cuts.

DANNY   From cuts?

LIAM   Yeah.

DANNY   And how did you help him, what did you do?

HELEN   Why are you asking that?

DANNY   So we know what he did.

HELEN   Is that important?

DANNY   It might be.

HELEN   Liam, what did you do?

LIAM   I shook him and said 'Mate, mate?' Like that.

DANNY   You shook him?

LIAM   Yeah, I shook him, I shook, I was just shaking him, but gently like, you know, and maybe a bit harder, because I was getting panicky

DANNY   How hard did you shake him?

HELEN   He was trying to help, Danny.

DANNY   I'm just trying to establish

HELEN   Okay, but please don't give him the second degree

DANNY   I'm not giving him the second –

         Liam, sorry, I'm not giving you the second –

HELEN   Where did the cuts come from?

LIAM   Knives.

DANNY   Knives? Someone cut him with knives?

LIAM   On his chest and face and around his arms, like… slices

DANNY   Fuck!

LIAM   I think, I mean I dunno, maybe they weren't cuts, maybe they were… tears or something, rips

DANNY   Not stabbed him? They cut him? They've sliced, they've actually…?

HELEN   Was there anyone around, were you alone?

DANNY   With knives?

LIAM   I was alone, I was completely

         I hugged him. Sorry.

             Beat.

DANNY   Was he conscious?

LIAM   No

DANNY   He wasn't conscious?

LIAM   Yes.

DANNY   He was unconscious?

HELEN   Well if he wasn't conscious, Danny…

LIAM   Yeah, he was unconscious.

DANNY   Fuck.

HELEN   Why did you hug him?

LIAM   Coz…he was hurt. Sorry.

DANNY   Jesus Christ! People have cut him with knives. They've literally cut him with knives and left him there, unconscious.

HELEN   Where was this?

LIAM   Markham Street. I mean round the corner.

DANNY   They've literally cut him with knives on Markham Street and left him unconscious.

LIAM   I was coming back from Ian's.

HELEN   What were you doing at Ian's?

LIAM   I just went to say Hello.

HELEN   I thought you didn't like Ian?

LIAM   I just went to say hello.

HELEN   I thought you hated Ian?

LIAM   Yeah, he's a cunt.

          This place, Helen. They do what they want. They run fucking riot. I'm scared to get the bus. Look what happened to Danny.

DANNY   That was nothing. Kids, just, you know, kids or…

LIAM   It's terrifying

HELEN   Is he still there?

LIAM   Who?

HELEN   The lad. Is he still there? lying there, bleeding…?

DANNY   Liam, is the lad still there?

LIAM   He's gone.

DANNY   What, he just got up?

HELEN   What are you saying?

DANNY   I'm asking, I'm just

HELEN   You sound like you're cross examining

DANNY   No, fuck, sorry, I didn't mean to –

          Fuck, sorry, Liam, I'm asking, I'm just

LIAM   Yeah, he just got up and went.

DANNY   But you said he was unconscious

HELEN   Danny!

LIAM   yeah, he just like, fucking, like a bolt, he just bolted
          up, he just bolted up and, you know, he bolted off.

DANNY   What he just got up and ran off?

HELEN   What is the matter with you?

DANNY   I'm trying to establish

HELEN   you're not fucking Petrocelli

LIAM   he was just, like a bolt, Danny, he just bolted up,
          and he stared at me and he was covered in blood
          and his eyes were mad and ran off. He never said
          one fucking word, he just ran off.
          I feel really… I feel quite bad, actually

          I think you should move, Helen. You know. Shane
          and that.

          *Beat. Suddenly HELEN pulls at LIAM's tops, yanking it
          up and beginning to examine his body for marks. LIAM
          lets her do this, and DANNY just watches. Satisfied that
          he is okay, she lets him go. Beat.*

DANNY Did you call anyone? The police, or…

LIAM My phone's off

DANNY an ambulance or –

You're phone's off?

LIAM No, not off, Danny, no, not fucking

DANNY You're phone was off?

LIAM off, no, Danny, not off,

DANNY Couldn't you turn your phone on?

LIAM I mean gone, flat like, you know, my phone was, the thing was there was no juice in the

HELEN His battery was dead, Danny.

LIAM Dead, yes, thank you. My battery was dead, Danny. Look I'll show you…

DANNY You don't have to show me Liam.

Beat.

LIAM I just wanted to, you know, help, but I didn't know what to do, I kept thinking what do I do, and I was thinking I should go back to Ian because Ian's done first aid, but I didn't want to leave him on his own, because Ian's a cunt anyway and because he's a person, you know, he's like a person, lying there and you can't leave a person, just lying, in the street, lying on the ground, on the tarmac

DANNY This is insane, are you okay?

LIAM Yeah, yeah, no, I'm alright. Actually. I'm fine. I'm fine, actually, yeah, this is

He is crying, though he tries not to.

No, I'm…

DANNY   Liam?

LIAM   Ahhh, shit. Shit, shit, shit, look at me, look at this,
           you're having dinner, celebration, celebratory,

HELEN   we're not celebrating, we're just

LIAM   and I'm coming in like some sort of

HELEN   Don't worry about that, Liam.

DANNY   Liam, do not worry about that.

LIAM   rice, and

HELEN   That's fine, Liam

LIAM   I think you should move, Helen. This area…
           Because out there…? Animals, not kids, fucking…

           He is crying.

           She goes to hug him, but he pulls away.

           Nah, nah, I got blood, I got blood all on me.

           Sorry, fucking tears, and, what a cunt.

HELEN   You're not a cunt.

LIAM   I am, I'm a cunt.

HELEN   You are not a cunt.

DANNY   You're not a cunt, Liam.

LIAM   Do you think I could have a hug, Helen?

HELEN   Come here…

LIAM   *(Pulling away.)* Nah, nah, the blood, the blood

HELEN   Alright, look, we're gonna get you cleaned

LIAM   This top's fucked

HELEN   You can wear one of Danny's, can't he Danny?

DANNY   Yeah, of course.

LIAM   It was a present from Jeanie. Jeanie got me this
             Hels, it was a

HELEN   I know, but we can clean it.

LIAM   Nah, it's fucked. I've fucked it

HELEN   You haven't fucked it

DANNY   Which one?

HELEN   'Which one'?

DANNY   Just take any of them, Liam. Any of them's fine.

LIAM   Thanks, Danny, thanks, you're –

             *He hugs DANNY. DANNY keeps him at a distance so as
             not to get blood on him.*

             Sorry. Sorry.

             HELEN takes LIAM off.

             *DANNY sits at the table. Looks at the food, hungry. Pokes
             at the rice with his fork. Puts the fork down. Considers.
             Decides. Lifts a fork-full of rice to his mouth.*

             *HELEN enters and he puts the rice down. She carries
             a blue top.*

HELEN   Are you eating?

DANNY   No.

HELEN   I'm gonna give Liam this to wear, is that okay?

DANNY   Yeah. Is that my blue one?

HELEN   It's your blue one.

DANNY   Don't give him that, Helen, give him the green
             t-shirt

HELEN   Why?

DANNY   Helen, please give him the green one, that's the blue one, that's new

HELEN   What green t-shirt?

DANNY   The one with eagle-star on it.

HELEN   it's in the wash

DANNY   Fucking hell, Helen…

HELEN   Eagle-star?

DANNY   Did you tell Liam you were pregnant?

Beat.

HELEN   Yes.

Is that a problem?

DANNY   No.

HELEN   Why is that a problem?

DANNY   We only found out on Monday, I mean shouldn't we wait until

HELEN   Shit, sorry, Danny. I mean

DANNY   three months or – no, no, Helen, I'm not having a, it's not a problem, it's a question, I'm just

HELEN   Sorry, shit, I just

DANNY   No, no, Helen, I'm not, its not a problem, I'm not

HELEN   I just needed

DANNY   having a go, or

HELEN   Someone to talk to.

Beat.

DANNY   Oh. Alright.

Pause.

HELEN Look, if you wanna eat something, just eat.

DANNY No, I'll wait for you.

HELEN Just eat.

DANNY No, I'll wait for you.

Pause. A moment.

HELEN Fuck.

DANNY I know.

HELEN Poor Liam.

DANNY I know.

Is he alright?

HELEN Yeah. Yeah.

I think so. What do you think?

DANNY Yeah, yeah. I think he's alright.

He's strong.

HELEN He's not strong, Danny.

DANNY No, he's not strong.

HELEN Thank you for this. You know, for being so…with all this

DANNY What? Jesus, no, I mean it's, it's Liam. I mean he's…part of us…

HELEN And sorry I'm a bit…you know

DANNY No, no, god, no, you're not, not at all

HELEN Oh, I am. I am a bit.

DANNY You're not, you're really, really not.

HELEN Well. Thank you anyway. I mean that, Danny.

Pause. She looks at the food. Touches him.

So much for our special evening.

DANNY   I know. Never mind.
            We should be able to get another in one when
            Shane discovers drugs

            Beat.

HELEN   Are you being sarcastic?

DANNY   No, it was a joke.

            She is staring at him.

            I was joking

HELEN   Sorry, Danny. Christ, sorry.

            She hugs him. He returns it.

            You should make them funny, then I'd be ready for
            them.

            They break the hug, but still close, touching.

DANNY   Why did you need someone to talk to?

            What, in a bad way?

HELEN   No, not in a bad way, Danny, I just needed

DANNY   Because you can talk to me.

HELEN   I can't talk to you.

DANNY   Why can't you talk to me?

HELEN   Would you talk to me?

DANNY   Yes.

HELEN   What, you would talk to me?

DANNY   Yes.

HELEN   If you, like, needed

DANNY   Yes, yes

HELEN   to talk, chat about, you would talk with me, would
            you?

DANNY   Yes, I would talk to you.

            Beat.

HELEN   Well that's not how most people work.

DANNY   What did you need to talk about?

HELEN   Have I done something wrong?

DANNY   No, no, god, I'm not

HELEN   telling my brother, did you not want me to, because

DANNY   No, Helen, of course, no, no –

HELEN   Good.

            Beat.

DANNY   Listen, Liam's going to be fine. We'll make sure he
            is.

            She smiles at him. A moment.

HELEN   I'd better give him the shirt. Eagle star?

DANNY   Yeah, the green one.

            I'll call the police.

HELEN   Okay.

            He goes to the phone.

            What?

            He stops. Looks at her.

            Sorry, what are you –?

DANNY   Calling the police.

HELEN   Right.

DANNY   I mean we've got to call –

HELEN   Oh yeah, course.

DANNY   Don't we, I mean we have to

HELEN   Oh, yeah, yeah. Course.

DANNY   Shall I do it while you're in there?

HELEN   Great. Why?

                Beat.

DANNY   'Why?'

HELEN   Danny, hang on, just give me a minute, Liam's in
            there –

DANNY   'Why?' Someone's been hurt.

HELEN   I know, but

DANNY   So we should call the police

HELEN   Just hang on, is all I'm saying, a minute,

DANNY   What for?

HELEN   is all I'm saying,

            look, don't do one of your panics, please, this is

DANNY   What?

HELEN   let's just think, for five minutes

DANNY   What's there to think about?

HELEN   because this is all a bit mad, and we're, you know

DANNY   Are you saying we should *not* call the police?

HELEN   No, definitely not.

DANNY   Is that what you're saying? Are you saying that we
         should not –

HELEN   I am definitely not saying that, that is something I
         am not saying, but I am saying can we just, for a
         minute, for five minutes, without panicking, without
         flapping think first, please.

DANNY   I do not flap.

HELEN   Because this is my brother.

DANNY   I know it's your brother.

HELEN   He's the only family I've –

DANNY   I know he's the only family you've got.

HELEN   Well don't say it like I'm boring you.

             Beat.

         They're going to think Liam had something to do
         with it.

DANNY   No they're not.

HELEN   They are, yes, they are, because he's always, he's
         unlucky, Danny, you know he's unlucky, he has a
         record because he's unlucky, and

DANNY   What are you talking about? They are not going to
         think that.

             Silence. She stares at him.

         What?

HELEN   Right.

         Right, okay, right. You know when you were in
         Miami?

             Beat.

DANNY   When?

HELEN   When you were in Miami.

DANNY   When?

HELEN   When you were in fucking, when you were –

DANNY   When? When? what time, I've been there three
          times, what

HELEN   The last time, the last fucking time, I'm talking
          about the last

DANNY   Well I don't know that, do I?

HELEN   Well why would I start a sentence like that if I didn't
          mean –

          The last time, Danny, the last time you were in
          Miami.

DANNY   Okay, okay!

          April.

              Beat.

HELEN   The time before that.

DANNY   November.

HELEN   November, yes, well when you were in Miami in
          November this thing happened and

          and the police came round, but

DANNY   What?

HELEN   No, no, it's fine, he was completely innocent, he was
          with me the whole time

DANNY   The police came round?

HELEN   so it wasn't anything, you know the way he stays
          when you're not here, you know how protective he
          gets, so he was here with us, so

DANNY   The police came round here?

27

HELEN   Yeah, but that's not important, it was completely a mistake, they said it was a mistake and everything's fine, but the thing is

DANNY   Not important? Why didn't you tell me?

HELEN   Because, it's not… Danny, you're fixating on the wrong thing, it's not about that

DANNY   Why didn't you say anything?

HELEN   Because Liam didn't want me to.

DANNY   Why?

HELEN   Because he fucking adores you and he made me promise not to tell you, but that's not why I'm telling you, so can I please tell you why I'm telling you, please?

DANNY   The police came round here?

        Beat.

HELEN   Look, the thing is, I mean the thing is they were on a mission. They were on a mission, Danny. Right, this bloke gets hurt and someone, some scumbag said Liam's name and he's not even there, no one thinks he's there, no one, but some scumbag says Liam's name and because Liam has a record, because he's unlucky, Danny, and yes, stupid, he's done stupid things but a long time ago, but they did not give one single solitary fuck, they were on a mission.

        You see you think, right, and I'm not criticising, but you think that things work out fair, but things don't. Not for people like Liam. They really don't. This isn't the fair world you think it is, Danny, and I'm not saying what you believe and think is wrong because I love you for that, but now is not the time for that, because this is now. They are going to think Liam had something to do with this.

Please. He can't handle this, not now. Please, Danny.

Pause.

DANNY   Liam's innocent, Helen. He hasn't done anything. He has nothing to fear from the police, he is innocent. There is a boy, out there now, hurt. We have to call.

Pause.

HELEN   You are so…

you are so fucking…

you are so…

DANNY   What, what are you –

HELEN   How can you be so, I mean Jesus Christ, how can you be so fucking naïve? How can you walk around like, you walk around like nothing in the world is and then these boys, these fucking boys! You know, and you go on as if they're innocent and its your fault, our fault for breath, excuse me for fucking breathing a fucking breath, I fucking…

DANNY   Jesus Christ, Helen, I'm-

HELEN   Alright, well let's not have this child then.

Beat.

DANNY   What?

HELEN   You know, if that's…how, if you're gonna be all, if that's what you, if that's you're thinking Danny, then what's the bloody point in, let's not bloody well, we, we, we shouldn't, into this world at all, then.

Beat.

DANNY   Helen…do you mean that?

Beat.

HELEN   What?

DANNY   Do you mean…?

HELEN   No.

DANNY   I mean do you, have you been thinking…?

HELEN   Yes.

DANNY   Yes?

HELEN   No. Maybe.

          I don't know. Maybe. Maybe yes. Maybe I do. Shit.

DANNY   Are you serious?

          Pause. She is thinking.

HELEN   Okay. Look, no we can't, that's not for now,
          because, Liam, I mean Liam is in there, so… Yeah,
          yes, okay, we can talk about, like later, because now
          we have to take care of

DANNY   Is this something you've been thinking?

HELEN   so, so, so I'm just gonna, because he's in there, half
          naked

DANNY   Fucking hell. Jesus fucking

HELEN   because I've got to give him the, because he's
          standing in there half naked so, alright, yes, I'm just
          going to give him the… Okay?

          She goes. DANNY sits back down.

          Looks at the rice. Thinks.

          LIAM comes in wearing DANNY's eagle-star t-shirt.

LIAM   Jeannie gimme that shirt. Helen said it'll be alright,
          d'you think it'll be alright?

DANNY   What?

LIAM   D'you think that'll come out, what gets blood out?

DANNY just stares at him.

It's just that Jeanie gave me that shirt. Christmas present, last thing she gave me, you think that'll just wash, just wash out Danny?

DANNY   Yeah, it'll probably just wash out, Liam.

Beat.

LIAM   Thanks for lending me this.

DANNY   You're welcome.

LIAM   What deodorant do you use?

DANNY   Er, Lynx, I think.

LIAM   Yeah, nice.

Beat.

You alright, Danny?

DANNY   What? Me? Yeah, yeah, I'm fine.

LIAM   You sure?

DANNY   Yeah, I'm

LIAM   You're having dinner and this turns up.

DANNY   Liam, you're always welcome, you know you are

LIAM   Yeah, but you know…

DANNY   We gave you a key, you know you're…

LIAM   And I appreciate that. I don't forget that

Beat.

You alright after all…that?

>*He makes a vague gesture. At first DANNY doesn't get it, but then…*

DANNY   What? Oh, yeah, yeah no it was just

LIAM   Fucked.

DANNY   Fucked, yeah, but

LIAM   I mean fucking hell

DANNY   Yeah, but you know, it's just one of those things

LIAM   There's nothing you can do. There's too many of them and they know that, the little cunts.

DANNY   They do, there was nothing -

LIAM   You're not less of a man.

>*Beat.*

DANNY   I know.

LIAM   Asians, were they?

>*Beat.*

DANNY   Well, some of them, but I don't think –

LIAM   No, I don't mean it like that.

DANNY   I mean I don't think that was

LIAM   Yeah, no, Danny, not at all, I mean that's all fucked that sort of

DANNY   a factor

LIAM   racial, I mean, no. Ian's like that and he makes me fucking sick. Giving it all 'The Asians this and the Asians that.'

DANNY   Yeah

LIAM   and 'I'd like to cut open a fucking nigger's stomach' makes me sick, Danny, makes me sick, that sorta

talk. Makes me wanna fucking hit him, actually, and
Ian gives it all that but he ain't exactly a big man,
cut open your stomach, see what you think.

DANNY   He's a bit of a prick.

LIAM   Yeah.

         He's a mate though, so…

              Pause.

         You wanna talk about it?

DANNY   What?

LIAM   You know. Talk about it?

DANNY   No. It's fine, Liam.

LIAM   I'm shaking.

DANNY   Are you?

LIAM   Yeah, look.

              He puts his hand on DANNY's forearm.

DANNY   Yeah.

LIAM   Fucking hell, eh?

DANNY   Yeah, you're

LIAM   Like a leaf.

              Beat.

         I tell everyone about you, all my mates. You're
         living proof of what you can achieve. You're
         brilliant. This area, though, Danny, you know. You
         should take Shane out of here. Man of the family
         and all that.

DANNY   Yeah, yeah. It's not that bad.

It's good for transport. And they're opening a coffee shop round the corner so –

LIAM   I hate violence. It makes me cry. Always has, you ask Helen. You ask her, you ask her about Brian Hargreaves, I cried like a baby when he got hurt. She saw me through that, she was like an angel, an angel sent from god, I used to thank god that he'd given me one of his angels for a sister, don't tell Helen that, but I did actually think that's what he'd done, Jesus, I'm just jabbering shit, sorry, sorry

DANNY   It's fine, Liam.

LIAM   I was so happy when you two got together. I was over the moon when she told me you were getting married. I cried when she said she was carrying your child. I always knew she'd make a great mother, she could've abandoned me, could've let them split us up, that's what they wanted, they used to look at us and think we could really place that girl, but that boy… I know that, Helen doesn't know I know, but I know. And she never once allowed that, and more than that, Danny. Never even entertained the thought.

            We're abandoned here. Government? Fucking left us to beasts, and that's not blaming it on the Asians, Danny, coz they're good people some of them, some of them are very, very good people, not the cunts that did you, or hurt other people, go around hurting, they're scum, they're filth, but some of them…victims. Victims of prejudice.

DANNY   Your hand.

LIAM   What?

            Realises. Take his hand away.

            Oh, sorry, Danny, sorry, I'm fucking… Brain's gone to shit.

Where's Shane?

DANNY   At his Gran's.

LIAM   Ah, shit, fuck, look at me. Gone to pieces, brain's gone all –

> *HELEN comes through with the top, soaking wet. She goes straight into the kitchen without looking at them.*

LIAM   D'you think it'll be alright, Helen?

> *But she has gone. Pause.*

Jeanie used to tell us these stories, you know, and they were shit like, you know, I mean they never used to go anywhere and afterwards we'd be like in fits of laughter coz she'd just told us this story that went fucking nowhere, fucking nowhere, Danny. Yeah. Like you'd get a bedtime story about a horse named Darby and basically it's a talking horse and it'd have an owner who'd take it to market and at the market he'd meet an old friend and go off for a drink and the friend would ask the owner if he needed a job and he'd say yes and they'd go back to this bloke's farm where they'd work together bringing in the corn and his wife would get ill but then a doctor would come and heal her, and that'd be the story, that'd be the fucking story and we'd be like in fits of laughter, but Jeanie, wouldn't get it, she'd carry on, and we're going 'but what about the talking horse' but she was never bothered like, she'd just carry on. She was an angel. We wished we coulda stayed with her. Kept in touch all those years.

DANNY   I wish I'd met her.

LIAM   Thanks Danny. Thank you for that.

You think it matters how hard I shook him?

35

Because you asked how hard, and, I mean d'you think –

DANNY   Liam, I think you were trying to help and your natural instincts wouldn't've let you do anything to harm him

LIAM   D'you think so?

DANNY   Definitely.

LIAM   Okay. Okay.

> *Beat.*

Okay.

> *HELEN re-enters. Long pause.*

HELEN   I'm not sure that calling the police will help.

> *Beat.*

Danny wants to call the police, Liam.

LIAM   Does he?

HELEN   When you were in there he said he wanted to call the police.

> *Pause.*

Well, did you say you wanted to call the police?

DANNY   I...suggested...

Liam, I suggested

LIAM   No, no, fair enough

DANNY   I suggested, Liam, because

LIAM   No, fair enough, Danny, you're right, course. We should, we should...

HELEN   What, call the police?

DANNY   We should, shouldn't we? Liam, I mean shouldn't we…?

LIAM   Don't you think, Hels?

HELEN   I don't know, do you?

LIAM   He was hurt.

DANNY   I mean what if it was us?

HELEN   It wasn't us.

DANNY   What does that mean?

HELEN   I'm just saying, it wasn't us, so what's the point in saying something was something when something wasn't something?

DANNY   Someone's been hurt, Helen! Someone has hurt another person. Someone is bleeding, someone is bleeding now.

HELEN   Someone who might be involved, for all we know.

DANNY   Involved? Involved in what?

        Beat.

HELEN   Right. Right. He got up and ran away.

DANNY   And that means he was involved in something?

HELEN   I don't know, I don't know, Danny, but there was violence. There was at least a violent thing that he might have been involved in, or might not, but just say he was and we call the police and basically put Liam through all that for someone who, well, who might be…well, dodgy.

DANNY   Dodgy?

LIAM   I don't think he was dodgy, Hels.

HELEN   I mean he got up and ran off,

DANNY   He was terrified!

HELEN   Exactly! He was hurt but he didn't stay there? What's going on, think, Danny, I mean Christ, what was he wearing?

DANNY   What's that got to do with

LIAM   ah you know

DANNY   We can't judge him on

LIAM   all the gear

HELEN   I mean round here? a lad, hurt? lying on the floor, wearing all the gear? what's he been involved in, what's he running from?

LIAM   No, Hels, I don't think, definitely, I don't think he was

HELEN   Because I tell you one thing, I am sick of this place. I am sick of the people I love, my people being subordinate to the people out there, people who basically do what they want, run around, calling me a cunt, yes, Danny, because that happens Danny, when I'm with Shane, Danny, bitch this, and bitch that and you just want to close your eyes?

DANNY   No, I don't want to –

HELEN   Show us your cunt, bitch, how's your cunt today, bitch, can I lick your cunt, bitch, show us your cunt you cunt. And you do nothing.

DANNY   What do you want me to do?

         Beat.

HELEN   All I'm saying is that Liam has a record. He has a record. I'm saying that the police are going to be suspicious.

LIAM   Are they?

HELEN   Of course they are

LIAM   Yeah. They might be suspicious.

HELEN   They're the police, Liam, they're paid to be suspicious. He has a record. He has a record, Danny, I'm asking you please just to think about that. There is a lad covered in blood and it's all over Liam's shirt

LIAM   You just washed it

HELEN   That doesn't matter Liam, there'll be DNA, that stuff never comes out, and how is that going to look? The first thing we do is try and clean the evidence

LIAM   Evidence?

HELEN   Yes!

LIAM   Does that look bad?

HELEN   Washing the evidence? Does that look bad?

DANNY   Then why did you wash it?

HELEN   Because it was covered in fucking blood!

And will it help? Will it help anyone? This lad, who may or may not have been involved in something, and I'm not judging him, I don't know him, but I know people like him. And who are we helping? Someone who gets up with these cuts of his and runs off into the night, running from something and we don't know what that is, will it help him to call the police? Liam gets guilty if you so much as look at him.

LIAM   I go bright red if I talk to the police.

HELEN   He tried to help. Is that a bad thing? Should he be punished for that?

LIAM   They make me feel guilty, the cunts.

HELEN For someone we've never met? My brother for some…lad we've never met?

    Beat.

DANNY It's a person. There is a person out there.

HELEN Not a person I know.

DANNY What do you mean I do nothing? What do you expect me to do?

    Pause.

HELEN If this boy is innocent I feel very sorry for him. If he isn't, then I don't. But I don't know him.

DANNY Is that what the world comes down to these days, then? Who we know and who we don't know?

HELEN Yes.

Yes, it does, Danny. Today. These days. These days that is exactly what the world comes down to. Who we know, and who we don't know. Sorry.

    Pause.

What I would like you to do…

What I would like you to do, Danny…

TWO

Later.

LIAM, HELEN and DANNY, sitting at the table.

LIAM is eating, tucking into the salmon and rice.

They watch. He eats, enjoying his food as if they weren't there.

Silence, just the sound of LIAM eating.

He finishes. Pushes back his plate

HELEN   What were you doing at Ian's?

LIAM   Ah, he's a mate.

HELEN   He's not a mate, Liam

LIAM   No, he's not.

HELEN   He's a bad influence.

LIAM   That was beautiful, Danny, that was

HELEN   He collects Nazi memorabilia.

LIAM   He don't collect it, he's just got some. Gets it off the internet.

HELEN   You shouldn't go round there.

LIAM   Yeah, he's got like loads, really sick it is, got like letters, jackets, canisters of zyklon B, it's sick, it's really sick. It's mad, it's really disturbed stuff, Danny, though some of it is amazing.

HELEN   You should stay away.

LIAM   I said to him, that's sick and he just laughed. Some of it is really amazing, though, he's got a Lugar with SS on the hilt

HELEN   That's sick

LIAM   That's what I say, it's sick, but it's amazing as well and he's getting into all modern stuff, got this machete, reckons it's from Rwanda, getting all into all stuff from Iraq and Afghanistan, reckons he's gonna get a severed hand from the Democratic Republic of Congo. Downloads all those videos, like violence, gang violence and shooting beatings and beheadings, jihadist whatnot, he loves all them sites.

HELEN   Were you watching them?

LIAM   No.

      Beat.

    Some of them are terrible.

HELEN   You shouldn't see him.

LIAM   I don't even like him, but he's a mate, you know.

    We was at school together, so.

      He gets up. Stands there.

HELEN   What are you getting up for?

LIAM   No reason.

HELEN   Why don't you sit down?

LIAM   Okay.

      He sits. Long pause.

    Can't just abandon people.

    That rice was lovely, Danny. Simple, just simple ingredients, that's what I love about your cooking: lemon, cracked pepper and a good olive oil – what could possibly go wrong? Just simple, Italian, it's quite Italian really, see I wouldn't think about that, I love cooking but I'm a vulgar cook, I'd put loads in, spices, herbs, oils, pastes, fucking shitloads, I make food like I'm mixing cement, I know I'm doing it but I can't stop, the only thing I can really make is chilli, I'm a vulgar cook, Danny. That was fucking beautiful.

DANNY   I can't believe we're doing this.

HELEN   No, well, we are. We've made a decision so let's –

DANNY   I know we've made a decision, I'm just saying.

       Silence.

LIAM   There's… There's a steam fair up the park, did you see that, Danny?

DANNY   No.

LIAM   Yeah. No, not now, next week, the weekend, they're having it like, there's posters up there, you know. Steam fair next week, sort of thing.

DANNY   Is there?

LIAM   Yeah.

       Beat. He stands up.

Yeah, it's good they do that sort of thing, they do a lot of that sort of thing in that park, it's good.

DANNY   What's a steam fair?

LIAM   I'm not sure, as it goes.

DANNY   Is it a fair?

LIAM   No, it's not a fair.

DANNY   Not rides

LIAM   No, I don't think so, I mean if it is I don't think it's very quick coz it's all steam.

HELEN   Why don't you sit down?

LIAM   Yeah, it's like steam things, just like big steam, like
            a steam tractor or a big fucking steam, engine, or
            something.

DANNY   Right.

LIAM   Maybe like a carousel, but like it's steam, you know,
            so it's not gonna go very fast.

HELEN   Why don't you sit down, Liam?

            He sits.

LIAM   Tea cups, you know.

HELEN   Tea cups?

LIAM   Yeah.

            No I mean if you sit in a tea cup or something.

HELEN   What tea cups?

LIAM   It's for the kids, you know them things, them rides,
            for

HELEN   No, I don't know

LIAM   for kids, where they're in a tea cup, carousel, you
            know the things.

HELEN   No, I don't know steam-powered carousels with tea-
            cups for kids.

LIAM   Well, I think it might be like that, I dunno, I'm just
            guessing.

            Pause.

            I was thinking of taking Shane.

DANNY   Oh.

            Yeah, yeah, he'd love that.

LIAM   Thinking of taking him at the weekend.

DANNY   Yeah he'd love that, Liam.

LIAM   Great.

HELEN   What are you talking about?

   Beat.

LIAM   Taking Shane –

HELEN   In the park?

LIAM   Yeah.

HELEN   It's in the park?

LIAM   Yeah, but it's –

HELEN   You're thinking of taking a five-year-old to a fair in that park?

LIAM   Yeah, but it's in the day, Helen.

HELEN   A fair? Kids hanging out and stabbing each other?

DANNY   It's a steam fair, Helen.

HELEN   You don't even know what a steam fair is, you're worse than him.

LIAM   It's in the day, it'll be fine, it's a family thing.

HELEN   He's not going up that park.

DANNY   It's in the day…

HELEN   Are you two insane, he's just walked in covered in blood!

DANNY   It's in the day

HELEN   No way.

LIAM   He'll love it, Hels, it's like these steam engines and stuff, it's a family thing, there's gonna be families there and –

HELEN   Do you want some coffee?

DENNIS KELLY

LIAM   No.

HELEN   Do you want some coffee?

DANNY   No.

        LIAM gets up.

        What are you getting up for?

LIAM   I dunno. I just feel a bit… Is it hot in here?

        I think I'll stay up.

HELEN   Sorry, I'm snapping, but…you know. I don't mean
        to snap, but…

DANNY   What time is it?

        HELEN looks to LIAM.

LIAM   My phone's dead.

        She gets up. Goes to her phone. Looks. Sits back down.

HELEN   Five past nine.

DANNY   Do you think he's alright? What past nine?

HELEN   Five past.

        Long pause.

LIAM   Fucking tense this, innit.

DANNY   Maybe we should go out and look for him?

HELEN   What, now?

DANNY   Yeah. Check he's

        I mean alright, we've made a decision and we're
        not calling, and I agree, I'm with that, but he's out
        there, maybe hurt, maybe, I don't know, so maybe
        we should…check.

HELEN   Out there?

DANNY   Yeah.

HELEN   Could do. Yeah, I suppose we could do. But…

         I mean the sun's gone down. It's dark…

DANNY   He's a human being. Whatever else he's done, he's a human being, and I agree, we've got to look after Liam and, and ourselves, but aren't we a bit responsible for

HELEN   Yeah, we are, you're right, but…

DANNY   our fellow, I mean isn't that what we hate?

HELEN   Oh we do, yeah, but

DANNY   fuck you and I'm alright Jack and all that old

HELEN   Oh, yeah, we do, definitely, hate that, you're right, but, I mean it's dark

DANNY   It is. But this is important.

HELEN   On your own?

DANNY   What? No, well I was thinking me and Liam…

HELEN   Liam can't go.

LIAM   I'm not going out there, Danny

HELEN   He's gotta stay away from it.

LIAM   I'm shitting it Danny, I can't go out there

DANNY   Right, right, fair enough.

HELEN   You wanna go on your own? At this time?

DANNY   Well…

HELEN   After dark?

LIAM   I admire that. After what happened to you

DANNY   Oh, just kids and

LIAM   Kids? Cunts.

DANNY   and I was a bit drunk, so…

HELEN   Maybe it's not a bad idea. To see.

DANNY   Yeah, yeah. Maybe.

        Which, which way did he go, Liam?

LIAM   Away from the shops.

DANNY   Right.

        Into the…

LIAM   Into the estate, yeah.

DANNY   Right. Right.

        Right.

            Pause.

HELEN   I think you should stay here with us.

DANNY   You're probably right.

            Silence. They wait.

LIAM   Tense.

            Pause.

        Shanie excited?

            No answer.

        Little brother? Bet he's excited. Or sister, could be, couldn't it, sister, little sister, that'd be lovely, I bet he'd love a little

HELEN   Don't say anything to Shane, Liam.

LIAM   What? No, no, if you don't want me to –

HELEN   I mean that, don't you say anything to –

LIAM	No, no I won't
HELEN	Don't you fucking say a word to –
LIAM	I won't, Hels, I won't!

       Pause.

       Why?

HELEN	Because…

       Pause.

LIAM	What?

       Beat.

       What?

       Hels? What?

       Pause.

HELEN	Look, we're not
	one hundred percent…about…

       Pause.

LIAM	What?
HELEN	It's just
LIAM	You're joking.

       Why?

       She says nothing.

       Why?

HELEN	I don't think this is the right time to discuss
LIAM	Yeah, course, sorry, no.

       Beat.

       Don't. Please don't.

Sorry, fuck, sorry. Sorry, Danny. Sorry, Hels, none of my business, none of my fucking, but don't, Hels. I mean Christ, you're such, you two are such great parents and Shanie's such a great little man.

HELEN   I don't think

this is the right time to talk about

LIAM   I'm so sorry Hels, I'm so sorry Danny, this isn't the right time to talk about this at all, and it's none of my, not at all

But I don't understand why? I thought you wanted more?

HELEN   Yeah, we…we do originally, I mean originally

LIAM   I thought that was the plan

HELEN   That was, yes, the plan originally, originally that was…

DANNY   Originally?

Beat.

HELEN   Look, nothing's decided, Liam, we haven't even, I mean me and Danny haven't even really, have we, properly yet, so. But we were thinking that maybe, with the way things are, the question is, circumstances, you know living here and, and, and giving up my job as well, that's definitely, and at the moment maybe that isn't the right…possibly.

LIAM   I don't understand.

HELEN   Look. We just think maybe this isn't the right –

DANNY   You.

Pause.

HELEN   What?

DANNY   You just think. Not we. You.

    Beat.

    I want it. I want our child. I don't understand why you don't. Why don't you want it?

HELEN   I…

DANNY   I keep touching your stomach. Haven't you noticed me touching your stomach? I keep touching your stomach because I want to touch it, him, her, I want to touch him or her, I want to touch him or her and I want to push love for him or her through my hand, through your stomach, through your womb and into our child so that he or she knows that he or she is loved.

HELEN   I didn't

    I didn't say I didn't want it.

    I said…there's a –

    you're not making this, Danny, this is –

    I said there's a…doubt.

DANNY   Why is there a doubt? Why do you have a doubt? I don't have a doubt, why do you have a doubt? Why do you now have a doubt about having this child with me?

    Pause. They are looking at her. Cornered.

HELEN   You want me to…?

DANNY   Yes.

HELEN   You want me to say, in front of…?

DANNY   Yes

    Pause.

HELEN   I'm not…

When I look at this, our life, or lives, here, I'm not, if I'm honest, one hundred percent that it is entirely working or working out to, or in such a way, as, as, as well as we might have

been led to believe that

expectations…allow.

    Beat.

DANNY   What?

HELEN   I'm, you know, I think, maybe this has made me think about

DANNY   Expectations?

HELEN   and on balance, looking at everything, and are we comfortable bringing another, and it's just a question, I'm not accusing and it's me, us, both, Danny, but the question is still there.

DANNY   Expecta…? What fucking question?

HELEN   Look.

    Alright, Danny, Look. I'm… I'm just not one hundred percent sure our life, its what we

DANNY   You

HELEN   thought it was going to be when, when, when we

DANNY   When you

HELEN   Danny, that's not helping, that really…

    Beat.

    Look, I'm, I'm not saying that we are

DANNY   You are

HELEN   That we are talking about

DANNY   that you are talking about

HELEN   I'm not saying that we are talking about.

DANNY   you're not saying that you are talking about

HELEN   ending, no, not at all, because we are

DANNY   You are

HELEN   You are such a piece of shit, you are such a piece
          of shit sometimes, sometimes you are such, such a
          fucking piece of…

          Sometimes I look at you and I fucking…

          I fucking…

              Beat. She sits.

              Silence. For a long time.

LIAM   You been up the grave?

              Long pause.

HELEN   Mum and Dad's or Jeanie's?

LIAM   Jeanie's.

HELEN   Yeah, I was up there…

              Beat.

          Not in a while.

LIAM   no, no, she won't mind, she knows how busy you
          are, and I was up there last week, so…

          What about Mum and Dad's?

              Beat.

HELEN   I've been meaning to.

          I was thinking of going next week.

LIAM   Ah, that's great, Hels, yeah.

HELEN   Yeah, maybe Tuesday.

LIAM   I could come with you if you like.

HELEN   Yeah. No, I've got an early on Tuesday, so

LIAM   Right

HELEN   Maybe, later

LIAM   Yeah, course

HELEN   Maybe Friday. Maybe I'll go Friday.

            You wanna come on Friday?

LIAM   Yeah. Brilliant.

            Beat.

            I always say hello anyway, when I go up I say hello
            for you. I say 'Helen says hello.' I tell them what
            you been up to.

HELEN   Thanks.

LIAM   They're so proud.

            They're so proud of you, Helen. You and Danny,
            and everything you are, you know.

            Long pause.

HELEN   I'm sorry, Danny, that was a bit, you know. But
            you…

            Pause.

            So it's a family thing? This Steam thing?

LIAM   Yeah, I think so, I asked the guy up there and he
            said it's just for the kids.

HELEN   Right.

LIAM   Yeah. He said it'll be full of families.

            Beat.

            Plus the odd dirty old man with a beard.

   Beat.

HELEN What?

LIAM What?

HELEN Is that supposed to be a joke?

LIAM What?

   Beat.

   Oh, no, not

HELEN Is that supposed to be funny?

LIAM No, no, I wasn't, I don't mean, not paedo

HELEN That's not funny, Liam.

LIAM enthusiasts, like steam

HELEN You said dirty old men with beards

LIAM I meant enthusiasts, not paedos

HELEN You said –

LIAM I meant steam enthusiasts

HELEN You said…

LIAM God, no, I'm sorry, I'm sorry, Helen, I meant like dirty because of the engines and –

   Ah, Jesus, what am I saying…

   I'm sorry, Helen, I don't know what I'm saying

HELEN It's alright

LIAM I'm all, look at me, I'm all

HELEN It's alright, Liam.

LIAM Is it fucking hot in here or what?

HELEN What time would he be back?

LIAM   Oh, it's a morning thing, have him back here by one.

HELEN   Right.

        Well, maybe…

            Pause.

        I think I'm meeting Sarah on Friday, but maybe we could go to see Mum and Dad some time the week after.

DANNY   So we're going to let whatever's going to happen to him happen to him. Because he's not one of us.

            They stare at him.

        No, I just want to be clear. Because if we're going to do this we should be clear.

HELEN   We're not doing anything.

DANNY   Because we've made a decision, haven't we. We've looked at the situation, accepted it, summed it up and made a decision to do nothing. Because he's not one of us.

HELEN   Danny…

DANNY   So if we choose, knowing that he's hurt – not by us, by someone else, but still – but we choose to do nothing and if he's losing blood and that's hurting his body, if that is causing damage to his system, then we are choosing to allow something that causes damage to his system and is that the same as choosing to cause damage to his system?

LIAM   Do you think it's damaging his system?

DANNY   I don't know Liam, that's what bleeding is.

HELEN   Why are you doing this? Don't, Danny, really don't

LIAM   I mean do you think he's in danger?

DANNY   I don't know, Liam. But just say that we knew he was going to die…

HELEN   For fuck's sake, Danny!

DANNY   No, I'm just saying that if we did know that, and we took a decision to let him die, then what sort of people would we be?

HELEN   He's not going to die

DANNY   because he's a lad, he's wearing

LIAM   I mean d'you think he's… How long does it take?

DANNY   What, to bleed?

HELEN   He's gone to a hospital, Liam, he's probably in a hospital right now –

DANNY   To bleed to death?

HELEN   Don't say bleed to death!

LIAM   But if he didn't, Hels, if he didn't go

DANNY   If he didn't we don't know, Liam, I mean how bad was he hurt?

HELEN   He got up and ran off!

DANNY   There was a lot of blood

HELEN   Danny, please

DANNY   I'm just saying

HELEN   I know you're just saying but you're winding Liam up and he's winding you up and together you're blowing this all out of proportion

          Beat. Pleading look from HELEN.

DANNY   Okay, right, okay; he's not going to die, this boy

LIAM   D'you think so?

DANNY   I don't know, Liam, but say he isn't. Alright? Say
         he isn't, but what if that's wrong? And what if he is,
         what if he is in fact going to die?

HELEN   Jesus Christ…

DANNY   And forget the courts and prosecution and charges,
         the courts, even if no one ever finds out that we
         do nothing, we deliberately did nothing, we took a
         choice to do nothing, and he dies, how do we live
         with that?

LIAM   because he looked hurt.

HELEN   You prick.

LIAM   because he looked hurt bad, actually, Hels, I'm a bit
         worried as it goes

HELEN   He'll have gone to hospital, Liam he will now be in
         a –

LIAM   What if he couldn't?

DANNY   well if he couldn't I don't know, there was a lot of
         blood.

HELEN   Danny, please don't, because this is too serious, to

DANNY   What? What's the matter?

HELEN   You know. You know what's the matter.

DANNY   What, is this not meeting your expectations?

HELEN   You are such a fucking coward

DANNY   Oh, here it comes.

HELEN   This is your answer? Is this your fucking answer?

DANNY   Yes. This is my cowardly answer.

HELEN   And you wonder why, if, you wonder why –

LIAM   But say if he didn't, Hels?

HELEN   Who?

LIAM   The Asian lad

>*Pause. Silence.*

HELEN   What Asian lad?

LIAM   What?

HELEN   What Asian lad. You didn't say he was Asian.

LIAM   Didn't I?

HELEN   No.

>*Beat.*

LIAM   Well he was

HELEN   You didn't say

LIAM   I didn't think

HELEN   Right

LIAM   it was important

DANNY   He was Asian?

LIAM   Yeah, but I didn't think

DANNY   You didn't say he was Asian

LIAM   I just didn't think it was, you know…

DANNY   Okay.

LIAM   Coz it doesn't really

matter, because I'm not really, you know, his colour, his creed, I'm not really, all that sort of, you know, doesn't bother, I'm not, I'm not –

Sorry, why? Why d'you think it matters, I don't think it…

He was hurt. He was a hurt person. He was a hurt Asian person Danny.

DANNY   Okay. Alright.

    Pause. Silence.

So what do you mean, 'if he didn't'?

LIAM   What?

DANNY   What do you mean 'if he didn't'?

LIAM   Well, you know…with that amount of blood, what if he didn't get up and run off, d'you think he would've been alright?

DANNY   What if he didn't run off?

LIAM   Yeah, would he be alright, d'you think

DANNY   Did he run off?

LIAM   Yeah, he did, but I'm saying if he didn't

DANNY   What, run off?

LIAM   Yeah.

DANNY   Did he run off?

LIAM   Yes, but

DANNY   So what does it matter?

What does it matter what would've happened if he didn't run off?

LIAM   It don't matter.

No, it doesn't matter, it –

Why? I mean…you know…

    Beat.

It's hypothetical

HELEN   Why are you being hypothetical?

       Silence.

       You're hiding something.

LIAM   No. I'm not, I'm not hiding

DANNY   Are you, Liam? Are you hiding something?

LIAM   No, I'm not, I'm not hiding –

       Pause. They are staring at him.

       I don't believe you're…fucking

       being like… For him? You don't even… I'm your brother, Helen, and Danny I thought we was, you don't even know what sort of person…

       Beat.

       Alright. Alright, he was, yeah, he was dodgy. Alright? He was a little fucking, a dodgy little, and that's not racist, but he was involved in all sorts. He was involved in –

       And, I'm not casting aspersions but all I'm saying is, right, alright, I'll tell you what, all I'm saying is you don't know what sort of person he is alright? I mean I don't either, fair enough, but you said, Helen, you said that he was probably, so it's me over him, I don't understand why you're taking the side of a

       dodgy…

       Pause.

HELEN   Did he get up and run off, Liam?

LIAM   Yes.

HELEN   Then tell me.

       Beat.

LIAM   Helen. I swear to you, on mum and dad's grave, he
            got up and ran off.

HELEN   Okay. Right. Okay.

            Pause.

            So what is it you're hiding?

LIAM   I'm not –

DANNY   What aren't you telling us, Liam?

LIAM   Don't start, Danny

DANNY   Why are you saying he's dodgy?

LIAM   He said it, okay? Happy? I didn't wanna say
            anything coz I didn't wanna say anything bad about
            him, but he told me, from what he said, piecing it
            together, fragments, he told me he was involved in,
            in stuff, indicated that he was involved in all sorts,
            and you don't know this world, Danny, you're a
            nice bloke and I like you but you don't know, not
            really, not when it gets, bad things, essentially,
            fighting and money and stuff like that. That's what
            he was involved in.

DANNY   He told you this?

LIAM   Yes.

DANNY   He just volunteered this information?

LIAM   He was hurt so, in a state of, and I was helping him

DANNY   He just came out and told you this stuff?

LIAM   Yes. Yeah, I'm saying…

            I pieced it together. Yes. From what he, ramblings
            and

DANNY   When did he tell you this?

You said he was unconscious. You said he was unconscious, Liam.

Silence.

Liam?

LIAM   What?

DANNY   You said he was unconscious.

LIAM   Yeah.

HELEN   So when did he talk to you?

LIAM   When he…

When he – hang on, hang on, okay – when he…

got up and ran off.

DANNY   No.

LIAM   No?

DANNY   No. Not then. You said 'he got up, opened his eyes, stared at me through the blood and ran off.'

HELEN   Were you lying?

LIAM   No, no, of course not, you're confusing me now.

HELEN   When did he speak, then?

LIAM   Before.

HELEN   Before what?

LIAM   Before, he, before, when I found him, he was talking, like

DANNY   But you said he was unconscious.

Beat.

LIAM   Alright, look, stop it. You're confusing me, so just stop and…

and…

Alright.

Beat.

I found him. He was unconscious. He wakes up and started talking but then he passed out again, which is when I got blood all on me, because I held him in my arms, I didn't want him to bang his head and I put him down and then, a minute, and then he gets up and bolts off.

They stare at him.

And that's what happened. And I don't, I can't explain why I didn't say it was like that but I didn't. Alright? I didn't. Are you gonna believe me? That's all you've got to ask yourselves.

Are you

going

to believe me.

HELEN   Liam –

LIAM   No. No Liam, because you're my sister and I'm telling you something, you are my sister and I'm telling you something. So, Danny, so Helen…are you going to believe me? Yes or no?

Yes or no, are you going to believe me?

Beat. Suddenly a phone goes off.

Cheesy ring tone.

No one moves.

Rings again.

Rings again.

Rings again.

LIAM takes it out of his pocket and turns it off.

Puts it back.

Silence.

He just come out at me.

He just, I was scared like and he, he just come out
at me like that and I didn't, I just lashed out. You
know, an impulse or, I think he thought he was
with his mates coz he's not a big lad, and there's no
way, I mean he's not gonna come out at me on his
own, I thought he thought he was, you know it's
an alley and he's come out at me, you know, to do
something quite bad, actually, to hurt, or rob, or,
just hurt, I was scared anyway coz it's dark that alley
and he just come out at me like a fucking, steam
train, Danny, you know. And I just turned and,
lashed, and, lashed out, and, caught him, and….
And he went down. And –

Beat.

I just kept hitting him. I mean I was crying, I was
crying but I was smacking him and pounding him
and he's on the floor, silent, not saying anything
like, and I couldn't work out why and I'm hitting
and hitting coz I'm shitted right up and I think I
might of, you know, started cutting –

Like, I had this blade?

Ian

He was showing me these little throwing knives
he's got, tiny, little heavy fat knives for throwing,
blade about an inch and a half long, but he keeps
them really sharp, like, and we're talking and he's
showing me other stuff and what have you and I
didn't know I still had it, til I saw the blood coming
out of these cuts I'd made with it.

On this boy.

I was so angry, I was just 'why d'you come out at me, you little cunt' and he's not answering, he's not saying a word, which is making me angrier, and I stop and there's, just like blood, blood, and he's unconscious. That's, that's why he's not said anything. He's unconscious straight away, like, and I was, I kept, y know…

Beat.

I hugged him.

Pause.

Hels? Hels?

Danny?

Beat.

Hels?

THREE

LIAM alone, anxious.

Sitting. Staring.

Sniffs T-shirt.

HELEN enters.

Pause. They stare at each other.

LIAM   You remember Brian,

Hels?

Brian Hargreaves? You remember him?

She doesn't answer.

You remember, at Shackleton, we was at, before we went to, we was, we hated that school, didn't we, we was always, you know, outside and. Year four they wouldn't let us be in the same class, would they. Would they, Hels, they wouldn't let us, not in the same class, I remember that Hilson, that cunt Hilson 'She's in year six, Liam. Helen has to be in with the older children' well fuck you, you beardy cunt, our parents have just been burnt to a crisp, so –

Beat.

Brian was alright, weren't he, you remember, Hels?

You remember him eating that stick? You remember that? A fucking stick, Hels, he ate a fucking stick! Big fucking stick off the floor. I mean who would eat a…

Beat.

Only one of them ever talked to me. The dirty gypo kid who eats sticks.

HELEN I remember.

   Pause.

LIAM Yeah.

  I was saying to Danny. I cried when he got beaten up.

  The violence. I just cried and cried and cried.

   Beat.

HELEN You mean when you beat him up.

   He looks at her.

  What do you mean 'when he *got* beaten up'?

  You beat him up. When *you* beat him up, Liam, when you beat him up, what do you mean –

  You smashed him to a pulp.

  You hit him with a brick.

  You broke his fingers, you pulled them back, you snapped –

  We had to leave school.

  I didn't hate that school, I loved that school. That was the best school we were at. We were never at a school like that again and we had to leave. I loved that school.

   Silence.

LIAM Danny alright?

   Beat.

HELEN Yes. Yeah, he's…alright.

LIAM Reckon he's a bit shook up.

HELEN No, he's fine.

LIAM   Feel a bit funny in this shirt.

            Sniffs it again.

            I've fucked up haven't I?

HELEN   Yes.

LIAM   D'you ever wish they split us up?

            Beat. She stares at him.

            No, do you, though?

HELEN   How can you say that?

LIAM   You'd've got a good family if they'd split us up.

HELEN   I've got a good family, we're a good family

LIAM   There's something wrong with me.

HELEN   You didn't mean it.

LIAM   I'm scared, Helen. What am I?

HELEN   You…you over-reacted, you just

LIAM   Are you getting rid of it coz of me, Hels?

HELEN   What?

LIAM   Am I destroying you? Am I destroying you and
            Danny?

HELEN   What are you talking about?

LIAM   Am I a poison?

HELEN   Liam

LIAM   Am I a cancer, am I a dirty cancer

HELEN   You are not a dirty cancer

LIAM   Are you gonna tell the police?

HELEN   No. No, god, Liam, of course I'm not –

LIAM   Is Danny?

            No answer.

            I'll drink bleach before I go to prison.

            Beat.

HELEN   You're not going to –

LIAM   Tell him that, tell him I'll drink bleach before I go inside.

HELEN   Don't manipulate me.

LIAM   I love you. I love you so much. I love Shane. I love Danny. But I really love you. I really, really love you

            I'm fucking shitting it. I'm shaking again.

HELEN   Sit down.

LIAM   Okay.

            He sits.

            DANNY enters.

            Pause.

HELEN   How is it?

DANNY   yeah, it's fine, she's gonna keep him for another couple of hours.

HELEN   Is he asleep?

DANNY   It's half nine.

HELEN   He should stay there.

DANNY   She doesn't want him to stay there, she's got a thing in the morning.

HELEN   But he's asleep…

            What did you say?

DANNY   I just said that we needed a few hours.

HELEN   That sounds like we've got a problem.

DANNY   You're right, I should've said your brother turned up covered in blood following an incident with a knife.

You know what's she's like, she doesn't ask questions.

HELEN   She's gonna have to wake him up now.

     Beat.

Sorry.

Thank you for that, Danny. Thank you for doing that.

     Pause.

LIAM   How's your mum, Danny?

DANNY   Yeah, she's okay.

LIAM   She alright?

DANNY   Yeah, yeah, she's fine.

LIAM   Lovely woman. She's got, got a great sense of humour.

DANNY   Has she?

LIAM   I thought so.

DANNY   Okay.

HELEN   I was saying to Liam that we're going to sort this out.

DANNY   Right. How?

LIAM   Sorry, Danny.

DANNY   How are we going to sort this out?

LIAM   I'm really fucking sorry. I'm poison, I'm a cancer, a dirty cancer.

DANNY   How are we going to sort this out?

HELEN   Liam wants to ask you something.

DANNY   Does he?

HELEN   Yes.

DANNY   Okay. What does he want to ask me?

LIAM   Right.

Danny, I am really sorry about all this, I mean you're, you, you're a nice bloke, a really decent, and you don't deserve this, you're not that sort of bloke and I really respect you and everything, you ask Helen, I tell my mates about you, I tell them what you're doing and how your work's going and…

    Beat.

I was wondering

what you were thinking of doing.

DANNY   Doing?

LIAM   Yeah. Like now.

DANNY   What I'm thinking of doing?

LIAM   Yeah, what are you gonna do? Are you gonna –

Are you gonna call the police?

    Silence.

DANNY   Liam, I'm not gonna call the police.

LIAM   I love you two

HELEN   See?

LIAM   I love you two so much

HELEN   See? I told you, I said

DANNY   Of course I'm not gonna call the police

HELEN   I told you, there's no need to worry, Danny's not, he's not gonna

Danny's not…

Danny is not going to –

Beat. Suddenly she hugs DANNY. *Clings to him, suddenly desperate.* DANNY *returns the hug, love between them.*

Continues. LIAM *doesn't know what to do. Goes to speak, doesn't. Waits… Waits…*

HELEN *is still clinging to* DANNY.

They break. She pretends she has not been crying.

HELEN   Great.

LIAM   Thank you, Danny.

HELEN   That's…

No, I mean good.

LIAM   Thank you so much.

DANNY   It's alright, Liam.

HELEN   Good. Great. No, that's good, that's…

LIAM   Thank you so much, I feel like crying.

HELEN   Don't cry.

LIAM   No, I'm not gonna cry, but I feel like crying, that's what I feel like.

HELEN   Great. Good. No, good, that's…

Good. Good.

Now we just need to sort out what we're going to say.

DANNY   What?

              Beat.

         What do you mean?

HELEN   Well, we need to sort out our story.

         If the police come here. And ask us.

         We have to say that Liam was here. With us.

              Beat.

DANNY   We have to say that Liam was here with us?

HELEN   Yes.

DANNY   To the police?

HELEN   Yes. Of course. Isn't that what we're talking about?

DANNY   No.

HELEN   No?

LIAM   No, Danny?

HELEN   Well, what are we talking about?

DANNY   We're talking about not calling the police.

HELEN   But if they ask?

DANNY   Are they going to ask?

HELEN   No, they're not gonna ask, they're never gonna ask, they're not gonna ask in a million years, but if they do ask…

         Then we'd have to say that Liam was here. All night.

              Beat.

         Danny?

DANNY   Look, hang on

HELEN   What?

DANNY   You're saying lie?

HELEN   Yes.

DANNY   To the police?

HELEN   Yes, to the police, of course to the police. Who else?

Danny?

DANNY   What?

> *Beat.*

Doesn't that make us

accessories, or

HELEN   Yes. Yes, it does.

DANNY   Jesus.

HELEN   Danny?

DANNY   This is going too fast.

HELEN   It has to go fast.

DANNY   Why are you so calm?

HELEN   I'm not calm.

DANNY   Can we just slow, please, can we slow things down
and

HELEN   No, we can't slow things down

DANNY   think, because

HELEN   we can't think we have to do.

DANNY   I mean isn't that, what you're talking about, like
aiding and

HELEN   Well, what do you think this is?

DANNY   abbeting, or – Not that, it's not that, this is not that.

HELEN   What, not calling the police? Not calling the police is not that?

DANNY   No, it's not the same as

HELEN   Yes. It's the same as.

DANNY   No, no, I don't think it's

HELEN   Yes it is, fucking hell, Danny, wake up, this is not a game, this is your family, yes it is exactly the same, don't bury your head.

DANNY   No, look, this is really serious, though.

I mean Christ, what, like in a court of law? is that what, are we saying

HELEN   It's not gonna come to that

DANNY   like under oath

HELEN   It's not going to come to that, but yes. We are. That is exactly what we are saying.

DANNY   I don't believe this. That is…serious, it's really, really serious.

HELEN   Yes, it is. It is really, really serious. So can you please decide how much your family means to you.

      Pause.

DANNY   No.

No, sorry, look…

fucking hell…

Look, I, no, no sorry, Liam, I mean Jesus Christ, this is one thing but that, you're talking about actually fabricating and maybe in a court of law and, Christ, sorry, no, I mean we have, this is our life. We have a child. We have jobs, we have a house, we have a child. No. Sorry, no.

    Pause.

HELEN   Are you saying no?

DANNY   Yes.

    Beat. She goes to the phone, picks it up.

What are you doing?

HELEN   I'm going to call the police. I'm going to tell them what's happened.

LIAM   Hels?

DANNY   Right, don't start being dramatic

HELEN   I'm not being dramatic

DANNY   because, look, don't start

HELEN   I'm not being dramatic I'm just calling the police and turning my only brother in to the custody of the law

LIAM   Er, Hels?

HELEN   because we either do something or we don't, Danny. We do one thing or the other, we don't do half a thing, because that's doing nothing or doing the other thing or worse, there is no half thing, there's only one thing or another, there's doing or not doing, there's having a family or not having a family, there's us and them, protect or don't.

LIAM   Hels?

HELEN   No, Liam, because I'm not having this hanging over our heads like some fucking, every minute of every day waiting and knowing that I have in my family, in my home, every day, every night, looking at it across the breakfast table, staring at it, watching it chewing.

LIAM   Are you serious?

HELEN   Yes. At least this way you tell them. You tell them, you admit, it'll be better for you. *(To DANNY.)* It's one thing or the other, Danny.

> *Beat.*

DANNY   Is this what you did when I was in Miami?

> *She doesn't answer.*

I don't recognise this. I don't know what this is.

HELEN   Are you going to help?

Are you going to help?

Are you going to –

Yes, this is what I did when you were in Miami because he was innocent, he's my brother and he was innocent.

You don't go out after dark anymore. You cross the street when you see a group of lads. You sit on the bottom deck of the bus and you stop talking when there are boys around. I need to know if you're a coward.

> *Beat.*

I hate living here, are we going to live here forever? I'm not frightened of doing things for my family. Liam would die for this family. He would die for us, he would lay down his life for Shane, he would willingly stop breathing to save you.

DANNY   I'm… I am not frightened of doing things for my family either.

HELEN   Are you going to help?

Are you going to help?

Are you going to –

DANNY   Yeah.

> *Beat.*

HELEN   Say yes then.

DANNY   Yes.

HELEN   Say yes, then.

DANNY   Yes. I'm going to help.

And I'm not a fucking coward.

> *Beat. She puts the phone down.*

LIAM   I love you two. I love you two.

I love you two so much.

I think he was one of the lads that did you, Danny.

> *Beat.*

There's no law out there. We're abandoned.

I love being here, coming here, you know that? I love being in this house, you two, Shane, walking in here is like walking in to, I dunno, perfume or like warm, a warm, I just love it actually. But going back out there is like walking into shit. Like walking into a soft wall of shit. Into fucking sewage, Danny. You imagine walking into sewage, Danny? well it's exactly like that, sometimes I wash the soles of my shoes, I scrub them with a nail brush.

I wanna be honest with you because you're so beautiful.

I followed him. I saw him ahead of me and I
followed him. He was just walking ahead of me and
I thought 'you little' and I followed him, close, just
to scare 'you fucking little' and he's frightened and
I'm thinking 'how'd you like it, you little fucking,
hurting people I care about?' in here lending
me your T-shirt, out the wash, but still, and I'm
screaming at him, you know, I've got hold of him,
been hitting him, hitting his face, and I'm screaming
into his face, you Paki, you Arab, you terrorist, you
fucking bin Laden, you beheading piece of, you
not-my-colour cunt, how dare you how dare you
threaten the people I –

   Pause.

I dunno what come over me

I'm not like that. I'm not a racist. I dunno why

I dunno why…

I just wanted to scare him.

I dragged him into Ian's shed.

Tied him up. Hurt him. Left him there.

He's still there.

He's tied up. He's scared. There's a lot of blood.

   Pause.

Brian Hargreaves started saying shit about you,
Hels. He said you was gonna leave me. He said
you'd asked them to separate us, begged them, he
said, said you'd told him, said you was gonna go
off, started saying all this shit about you, about my
sister, said you was gonna go off with some posh
family, said it was all sorted and you was gonna
leave me. He was saying shit about you, that's
why…

I love you. I love both of you, all of you.

I love the fucking smell of you.

Silence.

HELEN   Can…can he recognise you?

LIAM   Yes.

HELEN   He knows who you

LIAM   Yes.

HELEN   he knows who you are?

LIAM   Yes. I told him.

HELEN   Right.

LIAM   I wanted him to think he was going to die.

HELEN   Right.

LIAM   I showed him my driving licence, I wanted him to think

HELEN   So he knows who you are.

LIAM   Yes.

HELEN   Right. Right.

Beat.

LIAM   Helen?

HELEN   I'm…

I'm just trying to think Liam.

LIAM   Okay.

HELEN   Okay?

LIAM   Sorry.

HELEN   No, no, I just need to

LIAM   Yeah, yeah, course.

HELEN   Because this is, a bit, I just need to

LIAM   Yeah.

HELEN   We need, we should

          talk to him.

LIAM   Right.

HELEN   Explain…

          We should explain, er, have a

LIAM   Talk to him?

HELEN   a chat, talk, just to, er

LIAM   He's scared.

HELEN   Yeah, yeah, but if we talk to him

LIAM   He's hurt bad.

HELEN   Is he?

LIAM   Yeah. I think he needs a hospital.

HELEN   right.

          That was a bit, that was a bit stupid, Liam, showing
          him your

LIAM   yeah I know

HELEN   Because that's

LIAM   Yeah

HELEN   A bit

LIAM   Yeah. Sorry.

HELEN   No, no, but…

          Danny?

> *Beat.*

> Any…?

> Any ideas?

DANNY   Any ideas?

HELEN   Yeah, any…

> *Beat.*

> ideas?

DANNY   Did you hear what he just said?

HELEN   Yeah, but there's no point in

DANNY   A chat?

HELEN   We have to be

DANNY   A chat?

HELEN   practical, so don't start

DANNY   a chat, did you just say chat, did you just suggest having a chat with a tied up Asian boy?

HELEN   I know you're a bit shocked, but

DANNY   Are you fucking mental?

HELEN   you're surprised, this is, I'm surprised as well, and

DANNY   You fucking attacked this boy?

HELEN   angry, even

LIAM   Angry?

DANNY   You cut him with a knife, you tied him up, you tortured him?

HELEN   Alright, but let's keep this

LIAM   Are you angry, Helen?

DANNY   What was going on, how could you do that, how could he do that?

HELEN   Alright, what do you want to do?

LIAM   Are you angry with me, Hels?

DANNY   What do I want to do?

HELEN   Yes. What do you want to do, what do you actually want to physically do, when you've finished flapping, when you've finished panicking, and screaming and screeching like a child, like a little fucking girl, Danny, when you've finished thinking and fantasising that we can do nothing what do you actually want to physically do?

DANNY   Don't talk to me like that.

HELEN   Do you agree we have to do something?

DANNY   Do what?

HELEN   Well, for example, we could do nothing, we could leave him there tied up and he could starve to death.

DANNY   Why are you even saying that, that's stupid, that's –

HELEN   Or Ian'll come home – yes, it is, it's stupid – and find him and call the police or do whatever he does when he comes home and finds tied up Asian boys in his shed, is that what you want to do?

DANNY   Obviously not,

HELEN   No. So we have to do something, we have to do something to help, to help, just stop thinking of yourself, Danny, and help.

DANNY   Help who?

HELEN   Help the boy, the boy, help the boy who's tied up

DANNY   Did you hear what he said? He has to go to fucking hospital, he's –

HELEN   Yes, exactly, he has to – right, yes, that's good, now you're thinking, that's, hospital, exactly.

You're right, he has to go to hospital. We have to take him

DANNY   Take him?

HELEN   Yes, of course take him, he can't get there on his own, how else will he get there?

LIAM   Sorry about all this, Danny

HELEN   We can't call, that's out of the, that's an ambulance, that's the police, that's prison, we can't call

DANNY   He's gonna call the police anyway

HELEN   That's why I'm saying we have to talk to him.

DANNY   Who, the boy?

HELEN   Yes, the boy, we have to talk to him.

DANNY   Talk to the boy?

HELEN   Yes, we have to talk to the boy.

DANNY   And what are we going to say to the boy?

HELEN   We have to convince him not to say anything.

We have to talk to him.

We have to scare him.

We have to frighten him. For his own good.

     Beat.

What else can we do?

We have to make sure that he's not going to say anything, we have to make him think that we're going to

kill him if

DANNY   What?

HELEN   if he, yes, if he says anything, yes, yes, kill him, torture him, kill his family, whatever it takes to make him say it was a random attack.

DANNY   And how are we going to do that?

HELEN   You have to threaten him.

DANNY   Me?

HELEN   Well he's not going to be frightened of me, is he.

DANNY   Me?

HELEN   You can, no I mean, you wear something on your, over your head

LIAM   Ian gave me a balaclava

HELEN   a balaclava, you can wear a balaclava over your head and scare

DANNY   I'm not wearing a

HELEN   so he doesn't see you and so he thinks Liam's not just, not just an isolated, not just one person, not just on his own.

    Pause.

Danny, I don't think, not for one, not for one minute that what he did, I don't agree with that, I'm shocked, and horrified and, but let's leave that for later, one side, and now, because he is my brother and he did this terrible, stupid thing to someone who… was he one of the boys who hurt Danny, Liam?

LIAM   Yes.

HELEN   Definitely?

LIAM   Yes, definitely, he told me, he admitted it, he was
            one of those boys.

HELEN   You're sure? He wasn't lying?

LIAM   He wasn't lying. He was too scared to lie.

HELEN   to someone who hurt you. He did it to protect you,
            in some way, and no matter how misguided that
            was he was trying to protect you and now you have
            to protect him because he loves you and I love you
            and now we have to do something.

            We have to act to make it the best it can be for
            everyone.

            Please.

                Beat.

DANNY   I

            can't do that.

                Pause.

HELEN   What if it was Shane?

            What if Shane came home covered in blood.

DANNY   Shane is five.

HELEN   He's not going to be five forever.

DANNY   Don't talk about Shane coming home covered in –

HELEN   What if Shane's twenty, or eighteen, or sixteen, or
            fourteen and he comes home covered in blood?
            What would you do?

                Beat.

DANNY   Why are you asking that?

HELEN   What if it was Shane? Or

another child?

Beat.

DANNY   What?

HELEN   What if it was Shane, or…

or another child?

Pause.

DANNY   What other child?

HELEN   Another child.

DANNY   We don't have another child.

HELEN   No. We…could. We could have another child, if…

What if we had another child, and it was another child?

Beat.

DANNY   What if we had another child?

HELEN   Yes.

DANNY   And that child came home covered in blood?

HELEN   Yes.

DANNY   The other child?

HELEN   Yes.

Beat.

DANNY   I thought… I thought you didn't want another child.

HELEN   Did you?

DANNY   Yes. I did.

HELEN   Well.

nothing's been

decided. Yet. It's all

it's all up for grabs.

DANNY   Is it?

HELEN   I'm asking for your help. I'm asking for you to make up your mind.

       Pause.

DANNY   What if we had another child and that child came home covered in blood?

HELEN   Yes. What would you do?

DANNY   What would I...?

       Beat.

I would...

I would...

       Pause. Looks at LIAM. At her.

HELEN   Is this a family? Tell me. Tell me, is this a family?

       Beat. Suddenly DANNY goes into the bedroom.

       Silence.

LIAM   Is he...is he gonna help?

Hels?

       She doesn't answer him.

Is he? Is he, Hels.

HELEN   Don't talk to me.

       Beat.

you make me sick. You make me sick, you make me so fucking...

You piece of…

How could you, what kind of person, how could you bring in here…

Don't talk to me.

FOUR

Late at night. No one here.

DANNY enters, coat on. Stares at the room as if he doesn't understand it.

Calms. Goes to sit, but doesn't. Decides to go into the kitchen, but HELEN enters. She has been in bed, but not asleep.

Pause.

HELEN   Danny?

He opens his mouth to speak, but no words come out.

She stares at him. He goes to speak again, but instead goes into the kitchen. She doesn't know what to do. She waits.

After a moment he re-enters with a sandwich on a plate and a can of beer. Stops. Stares at her.

DANNY   I haven't eaten.

HELEN   No

DANNY   I didn't have any

dinner

HELEN   Yeah, no, you should…

He doesn't answer.

Where's…

Where's Liam?

DANNY   He's alright.

HELEN   Where is he?

DANNY   He's alright, he's gone to the grave.

HELEN   It's twenty past one.

DANNY   Said he wanted to see Jeanie.

HELEN   It's twenty past one.

DANNY   Yes.

HELEN   Are you okay?

     He can't answer.

DANNY   I haven't…

     I didn't have any dinner, so…

     Looks at the sandwich. Picks it up.

     Puts it back down.

     Can you hold my hand?

     Beat. She goes to hug him.

     No. Don't.

     She stops, doesn't know what to do. Holds his hand. Pause.

     He takes his hand away and uses it to drink the beer with. When he put the can down he doesn't take her hand again.

     I went up the park. Went to look at the poster, the steam fair. There's a picture of –

     it looks alright, it looks okay, actually –

     there's a picture of a big steam engine and a family, blonde, all cheesy, but maybe that's the point. You know like circus posters, old ones, families and kids, people smiling, I couldn't tell whether it was a shit poster or whether that was supposed to be the point.

     You know I kept looking at it and I thought

     Beat.

     is that the point, is that supposed to be…

Beat.

I stood there in the rain. For about an hour. I couldn't move.

She goes to hold his hand.

Don't touch me.

She stops.

He picks up the sandwich.

Can't eat. Puts it down.

HELEN   What did you do?

DANNY   I scared him.

HELEN   Do you want to tell me?

DANNY   No.

Pause.

Liam had tied him to this workbench, just this shitty shed at the end of Ian's garden, he tied him so that, I mean it was too small, the bench, for his legs. So they were hanging down, you know, bended at the knees and, and he had no

shoes on, and he'd tied him, like strapped him with rope and those bungee cord things and he had lots of, on his body, there were quite a lot of

cuts, on his body, there were lots and lots of –

He'd cut him.

Quite a lot.

Beat.

And his face was swollen. Like one side was like a balloon so that one eye was shut and the other was just staring like mad, a cow or something, just, you know, there was a lot of blood actually, speckles and spots, some of it was dried and black, I mean he looked like

a monster or something, a swamp

thing

or something, not human and I kept thinking why's he got no shoes on.

    Pause.

Oh yeah, and there were holes in him. Holes in his

flesh.

Where Liam had stabbed him with the knife.

It's this really small knife, like with this stubby little fat blade, but because it's small it doesn't go too far, it just breaks the skin, he'd been poking holes in him. Belly, arms, upper legs, lots and lots, actually.

    Pause.

There was one hole in his cheek and I could see where the blade had snapped a tooth, you know the force, a molar, I think, not an incisor, so it must've been quite, the force must've been quite, like metal on tooth, snapping and I thought 'that's painful'.

There was this weird smell, I kept thinking 'what is that? What is that smell?' it was, you know, excrement, yes, because he'd, the fear had made him, and I didn't know that really happened and the shed was, you know, musty, but there was something else I couldn't –

HELEN   Why are you telling me this?

DANNY   What?

HELEN   What are you…

What are you trying to…

DANNY   Why am I telling you this?

>*Beat.*

I screamed at him. I stood there in this balaclava and screamed into his face, 'tell me where you live, you paki. Not so fucking clever now, not so big without your fucking mates, you paki, you nasty paki, tell me where you live you nasty fucking paki.' I was like a fucking –

>*Beat.*

because he wouldn't, he was scared we'd hurt his family so he wouldn't tell us, he just wouldn't. We got the gun, we broke into Ian's house and got the Luger and pointed it at him. I pointed it at him and told him I was going to fire it into his eye and when that didn't work I smashed the butt of it into his cheek. I did that, me. That's who I was.

HELEN   And

and did he tell you?

DANNY   What?

HELEN   Did he

you know…

DANNY   Yes. He told us. We made him tell us what it looked like so we could be sure it was the right place, and then Liam went to check on it.

HELEN   Liam went?

DANNY   You think I was going to leave him alone with Liam?

>*Beat.*

So I just sat there. Staring at his feet. Listening to him crying. Just crying, you know. And in the end I thought 'I'll put his shoes on. At least I can put his shoes on', because I was, I was me again, I wasn't any more like and I felt, was feeling, and I picked up his shoes and I went to his feet.

It was petrol. The smell. Liam had taken his shoes off to pour petrol all over his feet, I think he'd tried to, I mean there were matches all over the floor, like from a book, but shitty ones, so, so he couldn't, they didn't work, the damp, so they wouldn't light, so that's…

You know.

Pause.

So that's, you know, that's good, that's a positive, at least….

HELEN   And

And is it okay?

DANNY   Is it okay?

HELEN   Was it…was it the place?

Pause.

DANNY   Yes. It was the place.

HELEN   Right.

And what did you do with…?

DANNY   We drove him into the woods, left him there, said if he told anyone we'd torch his house, lock up the doors and windows first so no-one would get out. He believed every word.

HELEN   So it's okay? Danny?

DANNY   Did you hear what I just said? Did you hear what I've just said?

HELEN   Yeah, but –

DANNY   He fucking tortured him. I fucking tortured him.

HELEN   Well, you know…

DANNY   What?

HELEN   He went a bit

            far, but

DANNY   What?

HELEN   Yeah, yeah, he went a bit

DANNY   Did you just say 'he went a bit far'?

HELEN   Because he, he thought, this person was not

            Danny, this is not a good person.

            Beat. He stares at her.

            No, no, sorry, I know how that sounds and I do not mean that as an, but I mean Christ. This person, right, was not, he was someone, and that doesn't mean he should be hurt, of course not, but he was someone who hurts other people. He was not a good person.

DANNY   What?

HELEN   He was… Danny, he hurt, he was one of the people who hurt…you.

            Beat.

DANNY   Who?

HELEN   The lad.

DANNY   What lad?

HELEN   The lad, the lad, I'm talking about the –

DANNY   What lad, there is no lad.

        Beat.

HELEN   What?

DANNY   There is no lad.

HELEN   Yes there is, the lad

DANNY   The man.

HELEN   who, you've just, you've just

DANNY   He was a man, he was a grown man

HELEN   been…

        Beat.

        What?

DANNY   He was a grown man, thirty, thirty-five -years-old

HELEN   I don't…

DANNY   He was a man, just some fucking man, some Islamic man, that's all, on his way home. Some man with a beard, he wasn't a lad, he had nothing to do with anything, he had children, he was scared for his children, he was at least thirty-five.

        Pause.

HELEN   What?

DANNY   I hurt him, Helen. I had a balaclava on.

HELEN   He was…

DANNY   I've always wondered whether I'd be good at that sort of thing. Enjoy, or…something, you know, whether you… And now I…

        I feel like I'm rotting.

HELEN   He was a man?

DANNY   Yes.

HELEN   Not a lad?

DANNY   No, no, not a fucking lad.

HELEN   Just a man?

DANNY   Just a man, just a man on his way home

HELEN   An Islamic man?

DANNY   Just an Islamic man on his way home to his wife and his children.

HELEN   Oh.

DANNY   Yes.

         Yes. Oh.

         Front door slams, really loud.

         Moment later LIAM enters.

LIAM   Shit, sorry, Hels. Sorry Danny, fuck. Sorry, I fucking let go and that door, I keep forgetting, I just, it slams, it…bit strong that door bit fucking –

         Looks at them.

         Pause.

         Alright, Danny?

         No answer.

         Hels?

         No answer.

         Yeah. Yeah, fair enough, that's…

         Sorry about that. Sorry about…well, I'm sorry. This is all wrong, I know it is and, and look I wanna say I'm sorry. Sorry, Hels.

Sorry, Danny.

Sorry, Hels.

They say nothing.

Okay, okay, alright. Fair enough, I'm not saying anything different, and I have to say that I don't feel good about bringing you, not at all, I do not feel good at all about, you know, you've got this world, this beautiful world and it's like dragging a dead cat into it and leaving it on your sofa, on your beautiful sofa that you got from John Lewis and saying 'look, look a dead fucking cat.'

But there are dead cats in the world, Danny, there are dead cats, Hels.

Beat.

You're pissed off at me, aren't you.

Okay. I deserve that. Alright, I deserve that, that is fair enough, but I'm gonna make it up to you. Hels? I'm going to make it up to you. I am going to make it up to you, Danny, I'm gonna make amends. There. That's a fucking contract. That is a fucking promise.

Pause.

HELEN   He was a man?

LIAM   Well

HELEN   Was he or wasn't he?

LIAM   Well, yeah, but

HELEN   He was?

LIAM   he looked, I mean it was dark and…

Beat.

Yes. He was.

HELEN   Why.

LIAM   I

dunno. I dunno, Hels, I just...

I dunno.

Pause.

HELEN   You don't know.

LIAM   No.

HELEN   Right.

DANNY   I don't want him in my house.

LIAM   Can I just say something? Can I just say one thing?
I look at you, Danny, I look at you and I want,
not to be like you, not to be you, but yes, in some
way actually to be you, to actually be in some way
a fucking part of you, but I want it to be me, I
want you to be me. And if you and Hels weren't, I
would still, and I look at you and I say 'Yeah, he's
had all the breaks, so what? He's got a family, so
what, he knows what he's doing, so what? He's
got a good job and mates that he gets on with and
a beautiful girlfriend, he's clever and he's had all
the advantages in life and that may well be why he
has all those things while another human being, a
different human being gets to have shit thrown at
them for years and then to top it all becomes a shit
human being in the process, so what: he fucking
deserves everything.' You deserve everything. And
I say good luck to you because you are everything
that man in this 21st century should be.

And I stand here, in your shirt, in your dirty fucking
old T-shirt that you pulled out of the wash to give
me and I feel privileged to wear it. I feel privileged

to stand in your stale sweat. And I see someone like
you and I can't help thinking that you should never
have experienced this, that your blissful ignorance
should be protected above all else, that I should lay
down my life to keep you in that state, but part of
me, Danny, and this is the part I hate, this is the bad
part, the dirty part, the part that I'd like to cut out
with a knife, part of me, and I'm not saying I like
that part, I'm saying I hate that part, but part of me
thinks you should be dragged down off that fucking
pedestal and be forced face down into the mud
so you can eat the same shit and rotting flesh I've
been eating, so that it gets in your mouth and up
your nose and that you choke on it. And I saw you
tonight, Danny. I saw you...

    Beat.

We're abandoned. There's nothing out there. It's
like they've all been beamed up to another planet
and just left us with the monsters.

HELEN   Get out.

LIAM   Right, Hels

HELEN   The monsters? You're the monster, get out.

LIAM   You're angry, okay, fair enough, but don't

say something you're gonna regret.

    Pause.

HELEN   Regret?

Don't say something I'm gonna regret?

LIAM   You're angry now, and fair enough, I'm not, not for
a second saying otherwise, but all I'm saying Hels,
is, I can be pushed as well, I have limits, there are
limits and all I'm saying, Danny, is it's been a long
and traumatic, so let's not –

HELEN   I was going to go with that family.

         Beat.

         Brian was right. I told him, because I was so excited. I had to tell someone.

         Beat.

LIAM   What…

         what are you…?

HELEN   His name was John, hers was Jackie, John and Jackie, they lived in a lovely place, I remember, green and I remember the road was…lovely.

LIAM   No, I don't…you didn't, this is, this is…

HELEN   They had a boy a little older than me, Adam, he had a tree house in the garden, but it wasn't in a tree it was on the ground, they'd built it for him on the ground because he didn't like heights but it was all his, they never went in there, they respected his space.

         Beat.

LIAM   Right, don't say…

         Okay, okay, fair enough, but don't say hurtful, Hels, things, Hels, because that's not gonna get us, where's that gonna get –

HELEN   She had a job, I don't remember what it was, but I remember she had it because mum never had a job, she just sat around smoking, he was a doctor and I thought that was amazing, that someone's dad could really be a doctor. And his face was lovely. He had a lovely face, I don't remember his face but it was lovely and their house was clean, not like our house, our house was filthy, I played a game with them, a board-game, I don't remember what it was, but we all sat down and played it together and I was amazed, all of us, just sitting there playing this game, John and Jackie as well.

Beat.

Adam kept showing me things. And telling me things. Things I didn't know, I didn't know them and he could tell I didn't know them but he never laughed at me, never once, he never once laughed at me for not knowing. He just told me things, all these things, and he showed me his rabbit. He let me hold her. She was soft and warm and I held her for ages, for ages, I just held her for ages, and I started crying, I was holding his rabbit and crying and he didn't say anything, he just let me, he just let me hold her and cry for ages and ages and ages and ages

LIAM   Right. Okay.

No you didn't, you're just

Beat.

I don't care, I'm not... Fucking hell, I mean, I'm not –

Anyway, that's not true, none of that is true, I mean none of that is –

What? d'you think I'm stupid? D'you think I'm fucking stupid, Hels? I'm not stupid. I'm not fucking stupid, Hels, I know what you're –

Beat.

I know what you're doing, I know, fucking stupid is it? fucking, fucking, none of that, not one word is true and you didn't, because you...

Beat. Suddenly takes a step towards her, so full of rage he doesn't know what to do with it. Wants to kill her, smash her face in, pound her to death. Stops. Masters it. Steps back from her.

She has not flinched. He has calmed himself.

You're angry. Yeah, and fair enough, you're, and so you're

being a bit, you are being a bit...

Okay, I'll take that, fair enough

HELEN   I loved them.

LIAM   deserved that, fair enough, can't argue with

HELEN   I begged them to let me go with them. But after you attacked Brian we got moved away. I begged and begged and begged.

LIAM   I forgive you. I love you and I forgive you.

HELEN   I don't want you to forgive me.

LIAM   Well I do. I forgive you. I forgive you so much.

The door swings open.

SHANE stands there, bleary eyed.

Beat. For a moment no-one knows what to do.

Shanie!

Shane almost sleep-walks into the room, going straight to Liam, arms around him, lying into him, half asleep. Liam, genuinely moved.

Ahh, look. Did I wake you up, Shay? Sorry about that, mate, that was the door, that flipping door again.

HELEN   What are you doing up?

LIAM   Ah, it's my fault, Hels, I woke him up.

HELEN   You should be in bed.

LIAM   You alright, Shay? You have a good time at your Gran's?

       SHANE nods.

       She's a lovely woman in't she. She give you ice cream?

       SHANE nods again.

       Did she! She's a cheeky monkey, in't she? Tell you what mate, you should get to bed, coz you're knackered.

       SHANE hugs harder into LIAM.

       Ahh, look. How about this; you go to bed and then on Saturday, if you ask your mum and dad very nicely and if you're a good boy, I'll take you up the park, would you like that? There's a steam fair up the park, it's all like engines and tractors and –

HELEN   Shane, come here.

       Beat.

LIAM   I'm just telling him about –

HELEN   He's not going.

       Shane come here, now.

       SHANE does as he's told.

       LIAM is shocked.

       It's late.

       Beat. LIAM gets up.

LIAM   Yeah. Yeah, fair enough. I'll just.

DANNY   Tell him to leave the key.

LIAM   Look, Danny, I'm –

HELEN   Leave the key.

LIAM   What?

                    Pause.

                Hels…?

HELEN   Leave the key.

                    Pause.

LIAM   Hels? Please don't tell me to leave the key.

HELEN   Leave. The key.

                    Beat. LIAM takes the key out of his pocket.

                    Puts it on the table.

                    Doesn't know what to do.

                Yeah, well, I'm a bit tired and…

                Bye Shane, I'm…

                    SHANE is too sleepy too answer, hugged face into mum.

                Yeah.

                    LIAM goes. SHANE waves at him, not looking up, but LIAM doesn't see it.

                    A moment, then the front door slams.

                    They sit. Together. Silence. SHANE is sleeping.

HELEN   Are you alright?

                    No answer.

                I could make something proper to eat. Do you want something proper to eat?

DANNY   I can't eat.

                    Silence, apart from SHANE's breathing.

                What do we do now?

HELEN   I don't know.

         Carry on.

DANNY   How?

HELEN   I don't know.

         We find things to do and then we do them.

DANNY   What things?

HELEN   Things.

         Good things.

DANNY   Good things?

HELEN   Yes.

         We could…

         We could help people.

DANNY   Could we?

HELEN   Yes. We could help people.

DANNY   What people?

HELEN   People who

         people who need help.

DANNY   Right.

HELEN   We could do that, that'd be a reason to…

         you know, dedicate our lives to…

         or something.

DANNY   Right.

         Long pause.

HELEN   I've been thinking. While you were out. I was here
and I was thinking about lots of things and I got to
thinking about you and me

and I think, I think I've been a bit…harsh

DANNY   Harsh?

HELEN   on us, yes, harsh.

DANNY   I see.

HELEN   I think I've been judging us and us together a bit
harshly and judging us by some standard that isn't
a real, for whatever reason, and maybe it's time to
grow up and use real standards and, and, and

DANNY   Right.

HELEN   and accept. And once I'd thought like that, once I
thought the word accept, I began to feel good.

DANNY   Did you?

HELEN   Yes. I began to feel good about our life, and about
our family and about what we are and who we
are and what we've made together, given the
circumstances, given the hurdles and hiccups and I
know this is going to sound mad, because of tonight
and everything that's –

I know this is going to sound mad, you're gonna
think I'm, but I began to feel warm. Here.

She puts her hand on her stomach.

DANNY   Where?

HELEN   Here.

Beat.

And I'm sitting there thinking this, all this is running
through my mind and suddenly I'm

and this really is going to sound, you're gonna think I've lost the, but I'm gonna say it anyway because it's what happened but you're gonna think I'm totally, but because of this feeling and these thoughts I…

Alright; I began to laugh.

DANNY   Did you?

HELEN   See? I told you. You think I'm mad.

DANNY   I don't think you're mad.

HELEN   Don't you?

DANNY   No.

HELEN   You sure?

DANNY   You just sat here on your own

HELEN   Yes.

DANNY   laughing?

HELEN   Yes. I just sat here on my own laughing, I just started laughing. I just started laughing, and that's terrible because of tonight and what you had to, god, I know, and I felt such

guilt, because I was, but then I thought, you know this is positive and positive things, I shouldn't feel guilt, I shouldn't

but I couldn't help it I just laughed because, I felt this feeling and I knew that this feeling was you and me.

Us.

You and me made me so happy that I laughed.

Pause.

I want this child. I want to have this child. With you

DANNY   Do you?

HELEN   Yes. I do.

DANNY   Really?

HELEN   Yes. Really.

DANNY   You want that child. With me?

HELEN   Yes. I do.

Pause.

DANNY   When I move my hand it feels wrong. When I open
         my fingers it feels, my fingers, when I open my
         fingers it feels

         wrong, it feels

         Beat.

         you know like when you've had a limb cut off, but
         you can feel it, still feel it, still feel it there, but it's
         not there, they say you can still feel it there like a
         ghost limb, it's called. I think it's called a ghost limb.
         But my entire body feels like that, my hand my arm,
         my legs my feet neck my lips my eyes, it all, it all
         feels… But it's all still there. It's all still…

         Beat.

         Is he sleeping?

HELEN   Danny?

DANNY   He's sleeping.

         Goes over to them, looks down at SHANE.

         He's sleeping. He's sleeping.

         Look at me, Helen. I'm not a coward anymore.

         Bends down picks SHANE up from her.

         He's sleeping. He's sleeping.

Starts to take him out.

HELEN   Danny?

He stops, back to her.

What about…

Beat.

What about the –

DANNY   Get rid of it.

Beat.

HELEN   What?

DANNY   I don't want it.

HELEN   You don't…

DANNY   I don't want that child. Get rid of it.

I don't want that child.

Get rid of that child.

HELEN   I…

DANNY   Take it out. Take that child out. Get rid of it. I want you to get rid of that child.

Pause.

HELEN   I…don't want to get rid of it.

He stands there, hovering, saying nothing. She waits.

Danny?

But he goes. She is left there. Alone.

END